An Introduction to
Caricature

COVER ILLUSTRATION
Georges Goursat 'Sem' (1863-1934)
'Le Massacre du Printemps'
from *Tangoville sur Mer. Everybody is doing it now!* Paris, 1913.
Nijinski is tangoing with Zacherie Astruc
Lithograph, coloured by hand.
E 225-1953

I
Robert Dighton (1752–1814)
'A Windy Day'—Scene outside the Shop of Bowles, the printseller, in
St Paul's Churchyard
Watercolour
32.4 × 24.7 cms
D 843-1900

An Introduction to
Caricature

Lionel Lambourne

Assistant Keeper, Department of Paintings
Victoria and Albert Museum

LONDON: HER MAJESTY'S STATIONERY OFFICE

Series editor Julian Berry
Designed by HMSO Graphic Design
Printed in the UK for HMSO

ISBN 0 11 290397 5
Dd 696424 C /65

Acknowledgements
I would like to thank Ann Buddle, Sally Chappell and Christine Smith for
their help with the photography.
L.L. 26.3.1982

Editors Note
All measurements are given with the height followed by the width.
In cases where a plate from a book rather than the artist's original is
reproduced the measurements have not been given.

HER MAJESTY'S STATIONERY OFFICE

Government Bookshops

49 High Holborn, London WC1V 6HB
13a Castle Street, Edinburgh EH2 3AR
Brazennose Street, Manchester M60 8AS
Southey House, Wine Street, Bristol BS1 2BQ
258 Broad Street, Birmingham B1 2HE
80 Chichester Street, Belfast BT1 4JY

Government Publications are also available through booksellers

The full range of Museum publications is displayed and sold at
The Victoria & Albert Museum, South Kensington, London SW7 2RL

Aubrey Beardsley (1877–98)
Caricature in the form of a coin of Queen Victoria as a Degas dancer.
Inscribed '*Fidei Defensor*—Degas'
Pencil, Pen & Ink
D. 10.3 cms
E 39-1948 Bequeathed by H. H. Harrod

The Distorting Mirror of Nature

ave we not all, at some time, entered a hall of distorting mirrors at a fairground? Within it, we can change ourselves into dwarves or giants, or make ourselves grotesquely fat or incredibly thin: a taste of divine power but we laugh because we can change our image at will.

The caricaturist's role, the rogue elephant of the visual arts, resides in fixing such images. To adapt Hamlet's advice to the players, the caricaturist should . . . 'hold, as t'were, a distorting mirror up to nature'. A mirror in which we recognise, in more permanent form, the follies of our own and others' behaviour. Having perceived in an over talkative or over rapacious politician a large mouth the caricaturist then captures the essence of the man on paper. Sometimes he goes even further and sees in the large mouth a resemblance to a monkey or a shark, and from this produces an anthropomorphic type, a startling correspondence which provokes laughter.

When did this strange art begin? Some would trace its origins back to the Egyptians, to the Greek painters of Attic vases, and to illuminations in the margins of Gothic manuscripts [plate 2]. Humorous art is common to all ages, but before the late Renaissance it tends almost invariably to be general, and not particular, directed at types rather than individuals. In a world in which magic and monsters were realities, visual satire remained circumspect. To draw the antlers on a cuckold's head, or asses ears on a fool, was fine if the subject was generalised, but dangerously akin to magic if specific.

After the Renaissance, with the awakening of a new interest in man as an individual, caricature—the comic distortion of an *individual* man—could begin, although

2
Letter 'h' from an English writing book of 1550, copied from an alphabet by the Master of the Banderolles
L 2090-1937

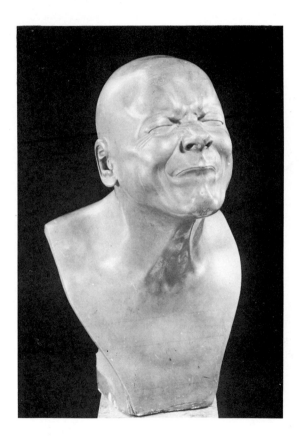

3
Francis Xavier Messerschmidt (1736–83)
Man Grimacing
Messerschmidt began a series of 69 heads of this type, based on his own features, of which 49 were completed. They were kept together until 1889 when they were dispersed by sale, but a number can be seen today at the Vienna Barockmuseum.
Lead bust
48.9 cms
A 16-1948

surprisingly we have no evidence of portrait caricature before 1600. Leonardo da Vinci (1452-1519), whose sketchbooks presage so many later developments in the arts and sciences, is often cited as the first caricaturist but his pages of grotesque heads reveal no intention to arouse laughter; rather a detached scientific interest in the sheer range of human ugliness. Nearly three centuries later a similar spirit of enquiry led the Austrian sculptor, Francis Xavier Messerschmidt (1736-83), to produce a strange series of self portrait busts which reproduced every variety of distorted human grimace [plate 3]. Such works of enquiry into the nature of the grotesque differ profoundly from the more satirical impulse which prompts caricature.

Due Filosofi.

4
Annibale Carracci (1560-1609)
Two Philosophers
This illustration was taken from Arthur Pond's *Imitations from Drawings—A Folio of caricatures after Italian Masters* 1739. Hogarth copied the heads of the philosophers in the border of his subscription ticket for *Marriage a la Mode* 1745 to illustrate 'the Difference Betwixt Character & Caricatura'.
Etching by Pond (1705-58) after Carracci
24.8 × 20.6 cms
E 4961-1902

5
Antoine Watteau (1684-1721)
Dr John Misaubin
Inscribed *Prenez des Pilules, prenez des pilules* and signed AP fecit 1739
Dr John Misaubin was a well known medical figure of the early eighteenth century, portrayed by Hogarth in *Marriage à la Mode* and *The Harlot's Progress* in the role of venereologist. Watteau, in this caricature, satirises Misaubin's over-reliance on the efficacy of pills as a remedy.
Etching by Pond after Watteau
28.6 × 21 cms
E 4964-1902

Prenez des Pilules, prenez des Pilules.
Dr Misaubin

Il Carnacci che canta nel Teatro di Valle nel Carnevale del 1748 il quale ebbe un Concorso di tutta Roma per il suo Modo di Gestire e di Cantare.

The First Caricaturists

It was not until the Baroque age of the early seventeenth century that the word 'caricature' (literally 'to load, to overload') came into use, and it was first used in relation to drawings by the most notable naturalistic draughtsman of the Bolognese School, Annibale Carracci (1560-1609). Why should this eminent painter of the great cycles of frescoes in the Gallery Farnese in Rome, the head of a large Academy dedicated to the revival of the 'Grand Manner', have been responsible, not only for the virtual invention of this type of drawing, but also for its very title? We are fortunate to have his own thoughts on the subject. 'Is not the caricaturist's task', he wrote, 'exactly the same as the classical artist's? Both see the lasting truth beneath the surface of mere outward appearance. Both try to help nature accomplish its plan. The one may strive to visualise the perfect form and to realise it in his work, the other to grasp the perfect deformity, and thus reveal the very essence of a

personality. A good caricature, like every work of art, is more true to life than reality itself' [plate 4]. Annibale Carracci's lead was followed by many artists in his immediate circle, among them Guercino, Mola, Carlo Maratta, notably Bernini and later the Tiepolos. But for all these men the production of such drawings was essentially an offshoot of their main serious preoccupation as artists. Their caricatures remained intensely personal private jokes, allusive references to subjective experiences of life, of the type to be seen in Antoine Watteau's drawing of Doctor Mead [plate 5]. The great French draughtsman's short life was clouded by ill health and tuberculosis, and the composition of this drawing may have afforded him personal amusement and relief from the continual medical ministrations to which he was subject.

The emergence of the pioneering figure of the first professional caricaturist was not to take place until the early eighteenth century, in the person of the Roman artist Pierleone Ghezzi (1674-1755). The son of a minor imitator of Pietro da Cortona, Ghezzi was originally a painter of altar pieces and other religious works. But it was his pen and ink caricatures, linear, sharply observed, often accompanied by aphoristic commentaries, which brought him fame. In these drawings, always with good-humoured wit, are reflected the Roman society of his day: the foreign noblemen, often accompanied by their tutors or 'bear leaders' on the Grand Tour, the aristocracy, artists and connoisseurs, the clergy, and the exotic figures of the famous castrati, whose pure and powerful male soprano voices were one of the most thrilling aspects of the contemporary operatic stage. Their extraordinary vocal range, temperamental personalities, and exaggerated costumes made them perfect butts for the caricaturist, and their widespread fame ensured the ready recognition of such drawings by the public [plate 7]. Of all Ghezzi's drawings these are perhaps the most remembered today, and stage personalities with their exaggerated emotions and gestures were to continue to provide ideal subjects for later caricaturists. But Ghezzi was also to widen the scope of caricature, from the narrow focus of individual personal caricatures of specific figures, to encompass wider social targets.

7
Thomas Patch (worked 1768-82)
Guiseppe Caramelli
Signed with monogram and dated 1769
From *Twenty-five Caricatures*, Florence, 1700
Etching
33 × 16.5 cms
V & A Library

8
Thomas Patch
Dr Sterne alias Tristram Shandy
Signed with monogram and dated 1769
From *Twenty-five Caricatures*, Florence, 1700
Etching
33 × 16.5 cms
V & A Library

Caricatura and Caricature: Italy and England

The Italian caricatures reproduced here have all been taken from a volume of etchings made by an Englishman Arthur Pond (1705-58), published in 1747. This work was most important in spreading a knowledge of Italian caricature to England where it had previously been chiefly known by verbal descriptions. In 1710, for example, Sarah Duchess of Marlborough, ousted from Royal favour by a rival, wrote to the wit Bubb Doddington, 'Young man, you come from Italy. They tell me of a new invention there called caricatura drawing. Can you find me somebody that will make me a caricature of Lady Masham, describing her covered with many sores and ulcers, that I may send to the Queen to give her a slight idea of her favourite'. With the publication of Pond's etchings, such commands could be readily translated into visual reality. Among the most notable early British experimenters in the new style was Sir Joshua Reynolds (1723-92). It is surprising to think of the highly serious Sir Joshua indulging in caricature, but as a young student in Rome he painted several satirical groups of his friends, and even a burlesque version of Raphael's *The School of Athens*, now in the National Gallery in Dublin. Later in his career he became ashamed of these youthful frivolities and re-purchased many, only to destroy them.

Far more at ease in the exercise of the caricaturist's art was Reynolds' fellow Devonian, Thomas Patch (1725-82), who spent much of his life in Florence (then as now a fine place in which to observe the affectations of art historians, or connoisseurs, as they were then more commonly called, and the extremes of fashionable society). Patch enjoyed satirising affectation with a zest which is peculiarly his own, and gave to his portraits of ecstatic dilettanti and nobleman with their muffs [plate 7] a memorable quality of 'high camp'. His eerie portrayal of the novelist Laurence Sterne [plate 8], which illustrates a passage from *Tristram Shandy* beginning 'and when Death himself knocked at my door ye bade him come again . . .' adds a new psychological dimension to the potentialities of the medium, which, though novel, had medieval antecedents.

The Morality plays of the Middle Ages, often performed outside the great cathedrals of England, were, as P. G. Wodehouse might have said, not strong on original plots. The virtuous, after vicissitudes, always triumphed, the wicked, after flourishing, always ended up vanquished by the Devil, to be dragged down into hell and its torments. But their stark moral teachings found a place in the popular political propaganda broadsides which formed a long-running commentary on the opposing forces of Puritanism and licentiousness in seventeenth-century English life. Such broadsides were often embellished with crude allegorical prints which owed much to the Dutch satirical tradition, and Charles I was moved to protest against 'these Madde Designs', particularly the illustrations which accompanied pamphlets criticising his conduct. The Civil War and the 'Bloodless Revolution' of 1688 led to the production of many such works, and even today their visual tradition lingers on the walls of Belfast and Londonderry in the symbolic representations of King Billy, the Protestant hero on his white charger. Crude journalistic hack work though such productions were, they established a public demand for pictorial comment on political events and social conditions.

The Shakespeare of the Etching Needle – William Hogarth

It was William Hogarth's achievements to sense this ready-made market, and satisfy it by the depiction of 'modern moral subjects', 'novels in paint', with which he founded an indigenous school of English pictorial satire. In his famous series 'The Rake's Progress', 'Marriage a la Mode' and 'The Idle and Industrious Apprentice', he takes up the stern tradition of the Morality plays and with techniques acquired from the Dutch genre tradition of Ostade, Steen and Metsu, turns them into serial sermons, in which Virtue inevitably triumphs over Vice. While these productions are his most justly famed works, Hogarth also commented on such evergreen themes as corrupt lawyers and politicians, the affectation of fashionable dress, and the iniquitous spread of foreign innovations.

Amongst such he included, surprisingly, 'that modern fashion, caricature', which he considered an aberration, a making of freak likenesses 'with any sort of similitude in objects absolutely remote in their kind'. Hogarth was here attacking, not the stylised likenesses of Carracci and Ghezzi so much as the anthropomorphic likening of man to animal, first described in G. B. Della Porta's famous study of 1586 *De Humana Physiognomia* (On the

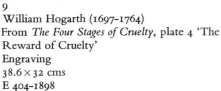

9
William Hogarth (1697-1764)
From *The Four Stages of Cruelty*, plate 4 'The Reward of Cruelty'
Engraving
38.6 × 32 cms
E 404-1898

10
Samuel Hieronymous Grimm (1733-94)
'The Macaroni'
Signed and dated S. H. Grimm fecit 1774
A dandy of the 1770s. In Oliver Goldsmith's *She Stoops to Conquer* 1773, Marlow, when his folly is revealed, exclaims 'I shall be stuck up in caricaura in all the print shops. The Dullissimo Macaroni'.
Watercolour
17.2 × 14.7 cms
P 39-1939

human face) which charted resemblances that led to the creation of the satirical zoo of prince turned into frog, lawyer into donkey. Hogarth had no time for what was to become a standard weapon in the caricaturist's armoury, preferring to reveal character simply through the face★. But the force with which he was able to do this enabled him to produce images like the anatomy lesson which forms the last scene in 'The Four Stages of Cruelty' [plate 9]. Here caricature is given a new and profound dimension that was to transform it from a minor branch of art into a weapon of universal application against the abuses of man by man.

★ Henry Fielding, whose novels mirror Hogarth's paintings of which he was an enthusiastic champion, discusses this point in the preface to *Joseph Andrews* of 1742.

How were Hogarth's works distributed, and what did they cost? The great sequences were sold by subscription, individual prints from 6d to 7s 6d, considerable sums in the money of the time, but still making them available to a wide section of the public, who formed a taste for collecting prints which lasted long after Hogarth's death. Prints were sold from shops like Bowles 'Map and Print Warehouse' depicted in Robert Dighton's 'A Real Scene in St. Paul's Churchyard, on a Windy Day' [facing title page]. What sort of prints, and what subjects, found favour in these shops in the second half of the eighteenth century, and who were the clients? We can in imagination follow the mincing steps of the 'Macaroni' dandy of 1774 [plate 10] depicted in the watercolour by Samuel Hieronymous Grimm (1734-94). In his fashionable daily lounge, he crosses St James

THE OPTIC CURLS·

OR THE OBLIGING HEAD DRESS·

CHLOE'S CUSHION OR THE CORK RUMP.

11
Matthew Darley (worked c.1750-78)
'The Optic Curls or the Obliging Head Dress'
Signed with the monogram MD and inscribed
'Published by M. Darley, 39 Strand, April 1, 1777
Engraving
35.2 × 24.7 cms
E 2292-1966

12
Matthew Darley
'Chloe's cushion or the Cork Rump'
Signed with a monogram and inscribed 'Published by
M. Darley, 39 Strand, Jany 1, 1777
This caricature is directed at the fashion for wearing
cork rumps (bustles) current in the 1770s. On the
projection of the lady's skirt lies a King Charles
spaniel. A 'Letter from a gentleman whose wife fell into
the sea but "it was impossible she should sink . . . she
owed her life to the Cork-rump the use of which I
recommend to all ladies who may love boating" '
appeared in July 1777 in *The Gentleman's and London
Magazine*.
Engraving
35.2 × 24.7 cms
E 2291-1966

G. M. Woodward Delin·   Preparations for a New COMEDY; or A Green Room in Town·   February · 1790·

13
George Moutard Woodward (1760-1809)
'Preparations for a New Comedy or A Green Room in Town'
Signed and dated February, 1790
Watercolour
32.3 × 48 cms
P 14-1931

Park, and walks up the Strand to no. 39, the Macaroni Print Shop, owned by Mat Darley (fl.1750-81), drawing-master, print seller, and caricaturist. Darley dominated the print market during the transitional period between Hogarth and the rise of Gillray and Rowlandson.

Caricature, towards the end of the eighteenth century, became a fashionable hobby, and among the 'Drol Prints, consisting of Heads, Figures, Conversations and Satires upon the Follies of the Age Design'd by Several Ladies, Gentlemen, and the Most Humourous Artists', our companion would almost certainly have enjoyed the spectacle of seeing some close acquaintance lampooned, or perhaps the more dubious pleasure of purchasing a caricature of himself. The technique employed in actually making these prints had changed from the

engraving method of Hogarth's day to that of the mezzotint, which enjoyed a brief vogue before the etched line used by Gillray and Rowlandson. The two examples of Darley's work seen here [plates 11 & 12] are representative examples of this type of print, an interpretative medium well adapted to converting the ideas of talented amateurs into saleable commodities by professional assistants. Some of these amateur talents were by no means negligible, and indeed added major innovations to the medium of graphic satire. For example, George, Marquess of Townsend (1724-1807), was the first to use portrait caricature in a political context, while H. W. Bunbury and G. M. Woodward in caricatures like 'The Green Room' [plate 13] brought a naive but deliberate crudity to play on sophisticated

THE WALTZ

14
Edward Francis Burney (1760–1848)
'The Waltz'
Signed Ed Burney Fecit London
Watercolour
47.6 × 68.6 cms
P 129–1931

themes with great comic effect.

One of the most interesting of these amateur artists—
of a slightly later generation but who may conveniently
be discussed here—was E. F. Burney, brother of the
diarist Fanny Burney, Mme d'Arblay. Just as we turn to
her diaries for a vivid picture of life in the court of
George III, so in her brother's watercolours *The Waltz*
and *An Elegant Establishment for Young Ladies*, we see
depicted the craze for waltzing, satirised by Lord Byron,
and the rigorous lengths to which girls submitted to the
dictates of fashionable deportment [plates 14 & 15].

While exaggerated fashions in dress and hair styles
were, then as now, staple subjects for visual satire, the
passion for foreign theatrical stars provided another most
popular target. One celebrated example was the society

craze for the two French dancers Vestris, father and son,
who were the talk of London in 1781, although England
was at war with France at the time. Their fame knew no
bounds, and the phrase 'Oh che gusto!' of the admiring
connoisseurs of their performance, served admirably for
the punning 'Oh Qui Goose-toe' of Nathaniel Dance's
humorous portrait, in which the younger Vestris dances
at his famous benefit performance, gaily waving a bag
of gold [plate 16]. Such artistic preoccupations at times
of national crisis are always open to criticism, and in
1803 Thomas Rowlandson was to portray 'John Bull
at the Italian Opera' [plate 17], an early appearance
of this patriotic symbol, who half a century later was
to feature in so much of Sir John Tenniel's work
for *Punch*.

15
Edward Francis Burney
'An Elegant Establishment for Young Ladies'
Watercolour
50.2 × 72.7 cms
P 50-1930

16
Nathaniel Dance R.A. (1734-1811)
'Oh Qui Goose-Toe!'
A caricature of Auguste Vestris (1760-1842). Inscribed
'He danc'd like a Monkey, his Pockets well cramm'd;
Caper'd off with a grin, "Kiss my A★★★ & be D—d"'.
16 May 1781
Engraving and mezzotint, printed in sepia
38.1 × 33.7 cms
E 4966-1968 Given by Dame Marie Rambert

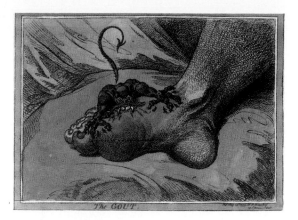

17
Thomas Rowlandson (1757-1827)
'John Bull at the Italian Opera'
Published 2 October 1811
Etching, coloured by hand
30.2 × 23.5 cms
23683.11

18
James Gillray (1757-1815)
'The Gout'
Published 14 May 1799
Soft ground etching, coloured by hand
29.8 × 38.2 cms
1232(9)-1882

19
James Gillray
'The Plumb-Pudding in Danger:—Or—State Epicures Taking Un Petit Souper'
Pitt and Napoleon cut up the world—the former with knife and Neptune's trident, the latter with sword and fork.
Published 26 February 1805
Soft ground etching, coloured by hand
25.3 × 35.3 cms
1232(x)-1882

The Golden Age of British Caricature

The perjorative sense in which Hogarth had used 'caricature' implying merely facile distortion, changed in the age of Thomas Rowlandson (1756-1827) and James Gillray (1756-1815). In their hands the medium came to full maturity. Both men employed the etching needle in their work with rare resource, and it was said of Gillray that he had etched enough copper plates to sheath the hull of a man of war. Looking at an etching like 'The Gout' [plate 18] one marvels at his mastery of the medium, his control of the bravura cross hatching, and the sheer venom with which the etching needle has skidded across the plate in wiry and expressive lines. Such technical virtuosity was harnessed to a visual

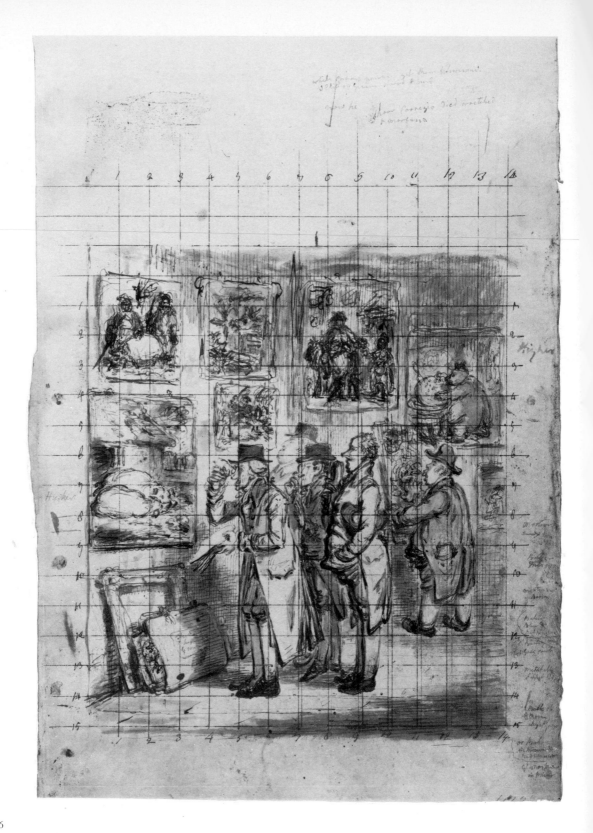

Connoisseurs examining a collection of George Morland's

imagination of compelling intensity, and his work enjoyed immense popularity. In 1802 a French emigrant described the scene outside his print seller's and publisher's window near St James Palace: 'The enthusiasm is indescribable when the next drawing appears; it is a veritable madness. You have to make your way through the crowd with your fists . . .'.

Such enthusiasm was caused by Gillray's masterly ability, sometimes prompted by political leaders but more often from his own imagination, to capture in his prints the essence of the latest national crisis or event in the momentous years of the French Revolution and the Napoleonic Wars. His portrayal of the British leaders such as George III, the Prince Regent, Fox, Sheridan, Canning and Pitt has preserved their personalities for posterity far more vividly than any state portrait, while his Napoleon, depicted as Little Boney, the Corsican Ogre, is a propaganda exercise of consummate skill. No historian of the period, to this day, can neglect such a brilliant summary of events as *The Plumb-Pudding in Danger: or, State Epicures taking un petit souper*. This 1805 caricature of Pitt and Napoleon carving up the globe is a subject which, like so many of Gillray's works, has often been redrawn to suit differing events by later caricature artists [plate 19].

He could also turn his attention to matters of artistic interest, and the V & A possesses all the preparatory drawings for his 'Connoisseurs admiring a collection of George Morland's', which repay careful study [plates 20 & 21]. The plate is a scathing indictment of the dealers who flooded the market with Morland's hack work and forgeries during the years immediately after the artist's death in penury.

'When etching he worked furiously, without stopping to remove the burr thrown up by the etching needle; consequently his fingers often bled from being cut by it'. 'Poor Gillray was always hypped and at last sank into that deplorable state of mental aberration which verifies the line . . . "How nearly wit to madness is allied".' These two comments by R. W. Buss and Henry Angelo, both men who knew Gillray well, chronicle the end of this most influential of caricaturists. After his death his work became virtually forgotten, for the niceties of Victorian morality did not view with favour the coarseness and sexual frankness of such works as his portrayal of the much caricatured Lady Hamilton [plate 22]. But in recent years, thanks to the magnificent biography *Mr Gillray, the caricaturist* by Draper Hill, a cartoonist, his true stature as the Prince of Caricaturists has been recognised.

The same criticism of coarseness was also levelled in Victorian times at Gillray's contemporary, Thomas

20 (opposite)
James Gillray
'Connoisseurs admiring a collection of George Morland's'
Gillray has made many interesting notes on this fully worked drawing; notably 'Poor Corregio died wretched, and Morland . . .'
Squared for transfer to the copper.
Black chalk, pen and indian ink wash
48.2 × 32.4 cms
Dyce 770

21 (above)
James Gillray
'Connoisseurs admiring a collection of George Morland's'
Published 16 November 1807
Soft ground etching
32.7 × 26.5 cms
1232(8)–1882

Rowlandson. He was certainly a man of great sensuality, whose uninhibited brush (he excelled as a watercolour artist even more than an etcher) recorded with amazing verve the physical aspects of his age, just as his almost exact contemporary and near neighbour William Blake recorded the spiritual. Two familiar anecdotes neatly summarise the man. As a boy, when a student at the Royal Academy Schools, he was nearly expelled for blowing peas through a pea-shooter at the posed life model. After inheriting, and squandering, a fortune in Paris by his early twenties he is reported to have said 'I have played the fool', and then lifting up a quill pen, 'here is my resource'. In thousands of vivacious drawings he captured every aspect of his time—military parades, rural fairs, royal processions, sailors roistering with their girls at Portsmouth Point, the theatre, Vauxhall Gardens [plate 23]—the list is protean in its scope. He has recently been the subject of many books, exhibitions and even films; a tribute to the remarkable animation of his drawings.

25
Thomas Rowlandson
Monkey Faces
Signed and dated T. Rowlandson
1815
Watercolour
31.3 × 23.5 cms
E 3678-1923 Bequeathed by
Mrs F. B. Haines

One aspect of his work has however been relatively neglected; his remarkable series of anthropomorphic studies. G. B. Della Porta's *De Humana Physiognomia* had been followed in the late seventeenth century by a similar work by Charles Lebrun. These theories were further developed by Johann Caspar Lavater whose *Physiognomische Fragmente* was published between 1775 and 1778, elaborating the doctrines into what he described as an exact science. With its aid, he claimed, one could 'know the inner man by the outer . . . apprehend the invisible by the visible surface'. He also developed still further the technique by which animal creation gradually approached the human form. While we do not know whether Rowlandson knew Lavater's work, it seems likely, and he was certainly aware of G.B. Della Porta, for actual copies of Della Porta's illustrations by him survive. In a number of physiognomical studies he was to experiment with similar comparative exercises [plate 24] in a fairly light-hearted manner. But in his drawing of a man's face emerging from a crowded sheet of simian studies, which might also be considered an eerie anticipation of Darwinian theories [plate 25], he provides a far more profound comment on the nature of man.

26
J. J. Grandville—Jean Ignace Isidore Gérard (1803-47)
The Cynosure of Every Eye
Engraving from *Un Autre Monde* Paris, 1844
V &A Library

Grandville and the Anthropomorphic Impulse

The most striking artistic development of Lavater's theories took place not in England, but in France, in the work of Jean Isidore Gerard (1803-47), who was known by the pseudonym 'Grandville'. Grandville took anthropomorphism to the limit of artistic expression, elaborating such apposite analogies as the anteater, with his long snout and tongue, as the customs official searching for contraband; the shrike as a human butterfly collector; and the centipede playing the piano, satirising the virtuosity of Chopin and Lizst. In his masterpiece *Un Autre Monde*, published in 1844, three years before he committed suicide, Grandville was to literally remake the world in a frightening assertion of the caricaturist's unique freedom of creative expression. Two representative plates from this book, whose strange fantasies so alarmed Baudelaire, show a Beauty in a box at the theatre who is literally the cynosure of an audience composed solely of eyes [plate 26], and the poetic image of fish fishing for men [plate 27].

21

LES POISSONS D'AVRIL.

27
J. J. Grandville
Fish Fishing for Men
Hand coloured engraving from *Un Autre Monde* Paris
1844
V &A Library

28
Honoré Daumier (1808-79)
'Répos de la France'
The obese figure of Louis Phillipe slumped on the
throne, from under which protudes three cannon, with
patent phallic intent. Behind the throne stands the
disconsolate figure of Marianne, while the Cock,
symbolic of Revolutionary Freedom, sprawls with its
neck awry—satiric witness to the oppression of Liberty
under the corrupt regime of the 'Citizen King'.
Published on 28 August 1834.
Lithograph
21.5 × 25.3 cms
Circ 143-1950

Philipon and Daumier

Earlier in his career Grandville had worked for Charles
Philipon, (1806-62), entrepreneur, publisher and caricaturist, who founded in 1830 the first comic weekly
magazine *La Caricature*, which was soon followed by the
daily paper *Le Charivari*. Both publications, illustrated
by the new and more easily printed graphic technique of
lithography, are the ancestors of countless comic papers
all over the world. Printed as newspapers, caricatures
could now reach a far wider public than was possible
for the single sheet prints of Gillray's day, distributed by
means of printsellers, clubs and coffee houses. Caricature
now took on a new role, with considerable social im-
plications. But this increase in stature incurred a greater
risk of censorship. Philipon, and the splendid team of
artists whom he gathered round him on his papers, all

LE VENTRE LÉGISLATIF.
Aspect des bancs ministériels de la chambre improstituée de 1834

at some time suffered fines or imprisonment for libel by the corrupt authorities of Louis Phillipe, the hated *Roi Bourgeois*.

Foremost among the Philipon team of artists, which included all the most notable French caricaturists, (Grandville, Cham, Gavarni and Doré), was Honoré Daumier (1810-79). He worked for Philipon all his life, producing some 4,000 lithographs, which are among the greatest examples of all satirical draughtsmanship, yet wishing every time he drew another caricature that it should be his last. Like Hogarth's, Daumier's art transcends caricature, reminding us that there are subjects too serious for tragedy. Two images must suffice as examples from many memorable scenes; his satiric portrait of the citizen King, Louis Phillipe in 'Repos de la France', [plate 28], and the obese figures of his ministers in 'Le Ventre Legislatif' (The Legislative Belly), shown in plate 29.

29
Honoré Daumier
'Le Ventre Législatif' (The Legislative Belly)
Most of the politicians depicted in this print, published in January 1834, were first modelled by Daumier in a series of powerfully characterised small clay heads which he kept by him for reference. Large prints like this were published to help pay for fines and legal costs.
Lithograph
43 × 28 cms
Circ 35-1950

Dandies and the Opera

Daumier's work in the 1830s shows a considerable knowledge of the caricatures being produced at the same time across the Channel in England. The years immediately after Gillray's and Rowlandson's deaths are usually considered to show a falling off in the quality of British caricature; but the productions of William Heath, 'Paul Pry' (?1795–1840), though in no way comparable in satiric force with the work of his immediate predecessors, have a charm which is all their own, particularly in his comments upon the vagaries of

fashionable dress, like 'La Poule' of 1827 [plate 30] and 'Hat Boxes' of 1829 [plate 31]. George Cruikshank (1792–1878), the most notable member of a family of gifted caricaturists, was in the course of his long life to range in his output from the 'Monstrosities of 1822' [plate 32] to his most famous work as the illustrator of Charles Dickens novels, notably *Oliver Twist*. The V & A contains a vast collection of drawings from all periods of his career. His contemporary, Alfred Henry Forrester, 'Crowquill' (1801–72), is also now chiefly remembered for his later Victorian work, but as a young man he left a spirited record of the 'Beauties of Brighton' [plate 33] in a watercolour of 1826; a promenade of notables etched by George Cruikshank, which include Talleyrand, Nathan Rothschild and the artist.

Alfred Edouard Chalon (1781–1860), one of the finest caricaturists of the period, is also extensively represented in the V & A's collections. Better known for his fashionable miniatures, watercolour portraits and lithographs of the Romantic Ballet, Chalon revelled in the atmosphere

30
William Heath 'Paul Pry' (?1795–1840)
'La Poule'
Published by T. McLean circa 1827
Etching, coloured by hand
25.1 × 36.4 cms
23689.7

of the theatre, and has left us some of the wittiest of all portrayals of the appearance of prima donnas in full voice, and the ballet dancers at unguarded moments. His incisive line, reminiscent of the Ghezzi tradition, was reinforced by a brilliant sense of colour. When we look at his watercolour caricatures made for his private amusement, we can almost hear the great soprano Pasta straining for a top note in *Norma*, the opera written for her by Bellini [plate 34], and enter backstage to see the make up session of a 'Prima Donna determined to shine' [plate 35]. His portrait of Violante Camporese singing a florid aria by Rossini at a concert, and wearing a fashionable hat, is particularly memorable [plate 36].

31
William Heath
'Hat Boxes'
Published by T. Mclean 14 July 1829
Etching, coloured by hand
24.4 × 35.1 cms
H. R. Beard Collection F 121.64 Theatre Museum

32
George Cruikshank (1792–1878)
London Dandies 'Monstrosities of 1822'
Published 14 Oct 1822
Etching, coloured by hand
26 × 37.5 cms
9481 D Given by Mrs George Cruikshank

33
Alfred Henry Forrester 'Alfred Crowquill' (1804–72)
'Beauties of Brighton'
Inscribed with the names of the people depicted,
notably the artist and his brothers on the left, Nathan
Rothschild right of centre in black, and Prince
Talleyrand on the extreme right.
Watercolour
22.2 × 38.2 cms
P 6-1932

34
Alfred Edouard Chalon R.A.
(1781-1860)
'Pasta' as Norma
Inscribed 'Norma, 1833—Pasta'
This and following caricature
depict the famous Italian Operatic
singer 'Pasta'—Giudetta Negri
(1798-1865) for whom Bellini
wrote *Norma*, first performed in
Milan in 1831.
Pencil and watercolour
45.8 × 22.2 cms
E 3328-1922

La Prima Donna determined to shine

35
Alfred Edouard Chalon R.A.
Madame 'Pasta'
Inscribed 'La Prima Donna determined to shine'
Pen and watercolour
19.1 × 26 cms
E 3317-1922

36
Alfred Edouard Chalon R.A.
'La Camporese'
La Camporese (1785-1839) was an Italian soprano who sang for Napoleon in Paris, and from 1817 in London. Her last appearance was in 1829 when her voice was worn. Her benefit concert took place on 12 June 1829 when this caricature was probably drawn.
Watercolour
33 × 22.6 cms
E 963-1924

Punch

Political caricature in the 1830s, in the hands of John Doyle HB (1797-1860), the founder of a famous family of caricaturists, became a surprisingly prim and proper activity, a process which was continued in the pages of *Punch*. This famous magazine, founded in 1841 in emulation of Philipon's journal *Le Charivari*, and today the longest running of all comic papers, gradually turned the practice of the caricaturist's art into a sober and respectable profession of a type which would have astonished Gillray or Rowlandson. This did not of course happen all at once, and in its early years the magazine possessed a raffish outspoken quality which filled a role similar to that occupied today by *Private Eye* or the recently departed *Oz*. These were the years which saw the word 'cartoon' introduced into the language in the modern sense of a humorous drawing. This

usage arose from a competition organised in 1843 to fill the walls of the new Houses of Parliament with frescoes depicting great moments in English history. The scheme was dear to the heart of Albert, the Prince Consort, whose Teutonic earnestness made him a favoured butt. The large rough designs, or 'cartoons', in the original sense of the word, were exhibited in Westminster Hall. John Leech (1817-64), one of the magazine's first great talents, saw the opportunity for a series of biting satires; the public remembered the word, and has clung to the new usage ever since.

As year succeeded year, and bound volumes of *Punch* became a staple feature of every English library, the magazine came to occupy more and more the role of comic chronicler of its age, and today its serried volumes afford us the most vivid microcosm of the Victorian period, an inexhaustible source of graphic social comment. Its contributors became a special breed of caricaturists, conscious of forming part of a great tradition, beginning with the fantasy of Dicky Doyle (1824-1883) son of John Doyle, who drew the original cover, but left when asked to draw anti-Catholic cartoons, passing on through John Leech to Charles Keene, George Du Maurier, and Sir John Tenniel, the first caricaturist to receive a knighthood. Tenniel's reign over the weekly lead cartoon lasted for half a century, and

37
John Leech (1817-64)
Mr Jorrocks 'Come hup! I say—You ugly brute!'
Published by Agnews in 1865
Chromo-lithograph
36.8 × 59.6 cms
E 3266-1953

38
George Du Maurier (1834-96)
'The Height of Aesthetic Exclusiveness'.
Punch cartoons in the late nineteenth century were
notable for the inordinate length of their captions. This
one, published on 1 November 1879, reads
'Mamma: "Who are these extraordinary looking
children?"
Effie: "The Cimabue Browns Mamma—they're *aesthetic*
you know!"
Mamma: "So I should imagine. Do you know them to
speak to?"
Effie: "Oh *Dear* no, Mamma—they're most *exclusive*—
why, they put out their tongues at us if we only *look*
at them!"'
Pen and ink
15.9 × 24.4 cms
E 396-1948 Bequeathed by H. H. Harrod

the nation nodded approvingly at his depictions of
statuesque Britannia clasping the hands of Marianne,
symbol of La Belle France, or Columbia, symbol of
America, or a stalwart John Bull waving a disapproving
finger at Germania or Erin.

The history of Punch is a subject in itself, which has
been ably told elsewhere, and the choice of representing
artists from it is an invidious one. But John Leech
(1817-64) must surely be included and his classic
illustration 'Come h'up I say, you ugly brute!' [plate 37]
for Surtees' Mr Jorrocks in his novel *Handley Cross*,
shows this spirited and underrated artist at his best.
After his early death in 1864, three volumes were
published of his *Sketches of Life and Character*, taken from
his weekly contributions to *Punch*, and to leaf through
their pages is by far the most instructive introduction to
the contemporary mores of High Victorian England,
for Leech's eye was everywhere from the servant's
hall to Rotten Row, from the fashionable Bond Street

lounger sporting luxuriant whiskers called 'Piccadilly weepers' to the coal heaver '' 'aving 'is photogruff took', from the crowded scene of Epsom Downs on Derby Day to the seaside.

George Du Maurier's canvas, while not so extensive, exactly mirrored the intellectual concerns of upper and middle-class society in the 1870s and 1880s. This was the age of the craze for collecting blue and white china and peacock feathers [plate 38] and of Norman Shaw's aesthetic elysium at Bedford Park, when the passionate poetry of Swinburne, the affectation of the young Oscar Wilde, and the classical beauties of Lord Leighton could all be satirised by Du Maurier in his 'intense' artistic family, the Cimabue Browns.

Vanity Fair

The most famous parody of the aesthetic period satirised in Du Maurier's caricatures was the well known Gilbert and Sullivan operetta *Patience*. We can catch a revealing glimpse of the famous composer [plate 40] and librettist [plate 41] in two portrait caricatures by respectively 'Ape' Carlo Pellegrini (1838-89) and 'Spy' Sir Leslie Ward (1851-1922). Both are excellent examples of the long-running series of such portraits which began to appear in the magazine *Vanity Fair* in 1862 and which later became a national institution. 'Ape', a friend of

39
'Ape' Carlo Pellegrini (1838-89)
'English Music'—Sir Arthur Sullivan
Chromo-lithograph
Published in *Vanity Fair* 14 March 1874
Theatre Museum

40
'Spy' Sir Leslie Ward (1851-1922)
'Patient'—W. S. Gilbert
Chromo-lithograph
Published in *Vanity Fair*, 21 May 1881
Theatre Museum

Sir Cecil Harcourt Smith
receives a deputation from
a Northern Town that is
meditating a Museum.

mx 1924

Degas, who commenced the series, was a comic portraitist of genius who conveyed not only a likeness of the subject, but the whole essence of their personality. 'Spy', his junior, who took over in 1873 when Pellegrini left *Vanity Fair* after a disagreement with the proprietor, was a more orthodox artist, but he excelled at his best in revealing, by close observation, the man hidden under the protective growth of Victorian whiskers.

The work of 'Ape' and 'Spy' was to influence considerably a far lesser draughtsman, but infinitely greater wit, the incomparable Sir Max Beerbohm (1872-1956). It was Beerbohm's great achievement to elevate this form of caricature synthesis into an aphoristic and devastating biographical summary of the whole career of the person portrayed; a cameo of character in action such as his depiction of Sir Eric Maclagen, (Director of the V&A) receiving a delegation of citizens from a northern town who are meditating a museum [plate 41]. His masterpiece 'Rossetti and his Circle' (the originals of which are in the Tate Gallery) remains to this day the perfect introduction to the Pre-Raphaelite group, who themselves had delighted in private caricature; particularly Sir Edward Burne-Jones who drew innumerable self-portrait sketches often in the company of his dynamic friend William Morris [plate 42].

42
Sir Edward Burne-Jones (1833-1898)
William Morris reading poetry to Burne-Jones, who sits bored by his side
Pen and ink
18 × 11.5 cms
E 450-1976

The 'Naughty Nineties' and 'La Belle Epoque'

'Black and white art is summed up in two words— Phil May', said Whistler. This aphorism, terse as a drawing by May himself, who never used six lines when five would do, does not exaggerate the stature of one of the most brilliant and endearing of Victorian draughtsmen. His series of *Annuals* which appeared from 1892 to 1905, give the whole range of his work, but his masterpieces are his *Guttersnipes* of 1896 and the *ABC* of 1897. In their pages the joys and sorrows of cockney childhood, later described movingly in the early chapters of Charlie Chaplin's autobiography, *My Life*, are given perfect visual expression [plate 43].

41 (opposite)
Sir Max Beerbohm (1872-1956)
'Sir Cecil Harcourt Smith receives a Deputation from a Northern Town that is meditating a Museum'
Signed and dated Max 1924
Watercolour
40.3 × 31.7 cms
E 1381-1924

43
Phil May R.I. (1864-1903)
'Lost'
Line drawing from *Guttersnipes* 1896
V&A Library

Just as May succeeded in capturing the essence of low life in the 'naughty nineties' [plate 44], so 'Sem', the pseudonym of Georges Goursat (1863-1934), was the perfect sophisticated chronicler of the sunny social scene at Paris, Deauville, Biarritz and Monte Carlo during 'La Belle Epoque', the first decade of the twentieth century.

'Sem's' caricatures provide the quintessence of 'chic' —the indefinably French quality of the 'in' joke of the glossy *grand-monde*. In his work the wheel of carica-ture comes full circle. Caricatures by 'Sem', like draw-ings by Ghezzi, portray amusing foibles of character instantly recognisable by both the subject and an inti-mate circle of associates. 'Sem' claimed he was never intentionally malicious, and his work could be enjoyed by the victim and his friends. They were produced in superbly printed Editions de Luxe, deliciously bound in stiff board covers with silk ties. The society they por-trayed was the small, brittle group of the wealthy and intellectual who met and remet, driving in the Bois,

44
Phil May R.I.
'With the Naked Eye'
Gorgeous Johnny 'Do you think your Missus will be able to *see* me this afternoon, if I call?'
Signed Phil May, 1902
Watercolour
19.1 × 16.5 cms
D 1341-1903

45
'Sem'—Georges Goursat (1863-1939)
Head Waiter and Guest—Penguin and Flamingo
From *Sem a la Mer* 1912
Lithograph coloured by hand by H. Saude
E 224-1953

racing at Longchamps or on the Côte d'Azur, in the years prior to the holocaust of the First World War. 'Sem' portrays the social round of lunching at a smart restaurant, and trekking to the casino as enjoyed by the middle-aged, while the more energetic younger set are shown on the dance floor enjoying the lascivious, insidious lilt of *the* dance craze of the period—the tango. In his 'Tangoville' [front cover] he satirises Nijinsky (in his costume of the faun in *L'Après Midi*) tangoing with Astruc. Elsewhere Forain (Sem's friend and the ferocious

caricaturist of the anti-Dreyfusard conservative right) tangos appropriately with Marianne, the French national symbol, and an English girl, suitably chaperoned, is dressed in a sort of Iron Maiden to prevent too close a physical embrace with her partner [plate 46]. Another favourite butt was the severely moustached figure of the Princess de Belboef, seen here [plate 47] being mistaken for a man by the doorman of the casino, a visual reminder of Colette's masculine Countess forever tapping out her pipe on the heels of her sensible brogues.

46
'Sem'—Georges Goursat
The Tango—Méthode Anglaise
From *Tangoville sur Mer*—Everybody is doing it now
August, 1913.
Lithograph coloured by hand
E 225-1953

47
'Sem'—Georges Goursat
'Chapeau! M'sieu S.V.P.'—the Princesse de Belboef at a disadvantage
From *Monte Carlo*
Lithograph, coloured by hand
E 77-1953

Years of Change

'Sem's' world, so confident and self-enclosed, was to shatter before the impact of the First World War, the rattle of the machine guns, and the heavy shells of the guns over the trenches. Sickened by the slaughter he never returned to caricature after the War. However the work of the caricaturist and the official war artist tended to overlap; for the grotesque, normally the exclusive domain of the caricaturist, became so much an everyday fact of life that the subject matter of Captain Bruce Bairnsfather's cartoons of 'Old Bill', the squaddie [plate 48], differed little from the devastated world painted by C. R. W. Nevinson or Paul Nash. 'Old Bill' became a symbol of the common man's involvement in the battlefield, and some of Bairnsfather's captions for his drawings in *The Bystander* notably 'If you know of a better 'ole, go to it' passed into the language, exactly capturing the spirit of ironical defiance which characterised the 'Contemptible little army' [plate 49]. An even more original humorous draughtsman during the War was William Heath Robinson (1872-1944) whose zany inventions added another word to the language. In one of his drawings both sides are stripped naked by powerful vacuum cleaners, an idea which may have been developed from Thomas Carlyle's satire on war 'Sartor Resartus', where two armies, stripped naked, are thus powerless to identify the foe.

Such innovative work did not, of course, completely supersede the allegorical style of caricature established by Tenniel, and continued by Linley Sambourne and Bernard Partridge (1861-1945). After a short and successful acting career, Partridge joined *Punch* in 1891, and during his long and distinguished service there (knighted in 1925) he caricatured every major political figure from the Kaiser to Hitler. His 'Appeasement of Tito' wittily adopts the style of Greek vase painting to comment satirically on the Balkan situation in 1915 [plate 50].

While *Punch* enjoyed its role as comic arbiter of British public opinion, German caricature from 1896 was dominated by the Munich journal *Simplicissimus*. The major contributor to its radical pages from 1902 was the brilliant Norwegian Olaf Gulbransson (1873-1958) whose ability to produce trenchant portraits in a few striking lines can be seen to advantage in his brooding image of his great fellow countryman Henrik Ibsen in the anthropomorphic guise of an eagle [plate 51]. Gulbransson's linear style was augmented by a highly original use of colour which added an acid sharpness to such works as his satire on the characteristic Teutonic theme of an aristocratic dog reluctant to be seen out

walking with its bourgeois, nouveau-riche owner [plate 52]. During the First World War, Gulbransson used yet again, and with great effect, the depiction of the British lion with its tail twisted by a German warrior, the cliché of an animal symbol as an immediately recognisable visual shorthand.

It's the Little Things that Worry
"It is an ancient campaigner and he stoppeth one of three"

48
Captain Bruce Bairnsfather (1888-1959)
'It's the Little Things that Worry "It is an ancient campaigner and he stoppeth one of three" '.
'Old Bill' hunting for fleas—a perennial problem for the 'squaddie' in the trenches.
From *The Bystander's Fragments from France*, Number 7—1918
Offset-litho
V & A Library

49 (opposite)
Captain Bruce Bairnsfather
'Sad but True "C'est la Guerre" '
From *The Bystander's Fragments from France*, Number 7—1918
Offset-litho
V & A Library

That attractive little village of Creme de Menthe groaning under the oppression of those hateful & degenerate Allies.

The village has now been relieved by a heaven directed German push — and all is JOY

Sad but True

"C'est la Guerre"

51
Olaf Gulbransson (1875-1958)
Henrik Ibsen
Hand coloured lithograph
From F. Blei: *Das Grosse Bestiarium der modernen
Literatur*, Berlin, 1922
V &A Library

50
Sir Bernard Partridge, R.I. (1861-1945)
The Persuading of Tito
A cartoon imitating a Greek vase painting satirising the
King of Greece and the situation in the Balkans,
reproduced in *Punch* 24 November 1915.
Pen, indian ink, watercolour
26.5 × 37.7 cms
E 448-1976

George Grosz
(1893–1959)

53
Georg Grosz (1893-1959)
Cafe Scene, 1916
Pen and indian ink
41.9×26.8 cms
E 3018-1938

With the end of the War the corrupt Weimar Republic, beset by racketeers, roaring inflation, and demoralised military forces exhausted by the titanic struggle, afforded the Berliner George Grosz unlimited targets for his savage analysis of a diseased society. On the outbreak of War he had enlisted in the infantry, and the death and destruction in the trenches filled him with rage, hate and the determination to hit back at 'the ruling order'. Twice hospitalised amongst severely wounded and mentally disturbed soldiers, he just saved his own sanity by pouring out his disillusionment into vitriolic drawings. A trip to the USSR after the War deepened his cynicism and disgust, and on his return to Berlin in 1922 he determined to forge his own style. Grosz's Berlin is a nightmare commentary on modern man, untinged by the sentiment with which Christopher Isherwood in his novels depicts the same scenes—the luxurious restaurants where the profiteers revel, the slums, the flop houses, the night clubs. In Grosz's own words, 'I made careful drawings, but I had no love of the people, either inside or out. I was arrogant enough to consider myself as a natural scientist, not as a painter or satirist. I thought about right and wrong but my conclusions were always unfavourable to all men equally' [plates 53 & 54].

Grosz's drawings appeared in two short-lived satirical journals *Die Pleite* and *Der Bluteige Ernst* which he founded with his friend John Heartfield, who in savage photo-montages attacked the emergent Nazi party. Both artists fled from Germany after Hitler came to power in 1933. In his turn, Hitler's Minister of Propaganda, Dr Goebbels, was to harness the power of caricature within the vilely anti-semitic pages of *Die Sturmer* and other Nazi papers.

54
Georg Grosz
'Des Volkes Dank ist Euch gewiss' (The People's
Gratitude is Certain)
Line drawing from *Die Pleite*, 1919
V &A Library

Des Volkes Dank ist Euch gewiß.

URGENT PREPARATIONS FOR THE WORLD FLOOD.

David Low

To turn from George Grosz's Berlin to consider the work of David Low (1891-1963) is to encounter a wit tempered not by Brechtian principles of alienation but by the sardonic, wry humour of the Antipodes. Low, a New Zealander, formed his style in the distinguished Australian journal the *Sydney Bulletin* before coming to England, initially to work on the *Star*. But he will always be remembered for his twenty-three years of association with Lord Beaverbrook's *Evening Standard*. Lord Beaverbrook's ebullient character made him a natural target, both for satirists like Evelyn Waugh and for caricaturists. Beaverbrook loved caricature and his newspapers were always distinguished for the calibre of the widely differing humorous artists whose work appeared in them; but the full measure of independence which he gave to Low, a Socialist, in the Conservative pages of the *Evening Standard* is virtually unique in the history of the medium. During the 1930s Low's cartoons were again and again to provoke anguished diplomatic protests from Hitler's Germany and Mussolini's Italy, and attempts were made by the

55
Sir David Low (1891-1963)
'Urgent Preparations for the World Flood'
In this cartoon for the *Evening Standard*, the name of the Ark, Queen Blimp, refers to the luxury liner *Queen Mary*, launched in 1936. Sheltering under the umbrella are Low and 'Joan Bull', while Baldwin, the Prime Minister, is the bearded figure with the pipe.
Crayon and wash
38.7 × 46.8 cms
E 530-1937

British government to suppress them, but press baron and caricaturist stood firm, and the resultant works have left to posterity a perfect epitome of the political mood of the mid-War years. Low's most famous creation was Colonel Blimp, the personification of reactionary 'old school tie' conservatism [plate 55]. After the War, when Low joined the Labour paper the *Daily Herald* in 1950, he was to pillory the innate conservatism of Labour in the figure of the TUC cart horse.

Caricature and Propaganda

During the Second World War caricature was to be used as a powerful weapon of instruction and persuasion. One artist to assist in the propaganda activities of the Ministry of Information was H. M. Bateman (1887-1970). He had achieved fame for his masterly depictions of such embarrassing situations as 'The young Etonian who was asked to play "Here we go gathering nuts in May" '. His poster, 'The Wife who squandered electricity' [plate 56], wittily conveys the reproving message of fuel economy. This poster was one of many similar exhortations to the public during the War years. One of the most irritating for blitz weary Londoners was the ubiquitous 'Mr Brown of London Town', the creation of David Langdon (1887-1965). The windows of Underground trains were then covered with a protective mesh to stop splintering glass, which also prevented passengers from looking out to see their stations. The mesh was frequently removed, leading Mr Brown to comment;

> I trust you'll pardon my correction
> That stuff is there for your protection.

One of the most famous graffiti in Wartime London was the scrawled rejoinder on the poster,

> I thank you for the information
> But still can't see the ruddy station!

Another famous war-time slogan, 'Careless talk costs lives', was used by Kenneth Bird, 'Fougasse', in his design for a small adhesive label to be affixed to telephones in those security-conscious years [plate 57].

56
Henry Mayo Bateman (1887-1970)
One of a series of posters entitled *Save Fuel to Make Munitions for Battle* issued by the Ministry for Fuel and Power to help the war effort, and published by H.M.S.O.
Colour Offset
74.6 × 49.3 cms
E 158-1973

57
Cyril Kenneth Bird, 'Fougasse' (1887-1965)
'Careless Talk Costs Lives—Maybe he's listening too'
Design for a telephone stick-on label circa 1940, with a caricature of Hitler.
Pen and indian ink
27.2 × 19.4 cms
E 172-1976 Given by Mrs. M. H. Bird, the widow of the artist.

43

Think, in this batter'd caravanserai,
Whose Portals are alternate Night
                              and Day,
How Sultan after Sultan with his
                              Pomp
Abode his destin'd Hour, and went
                              his way.

(Advt.)

The Newspaper
Cartoon

With the end of the War and the death of Sir Bernard Partridge in 1945, the long domination of caricature by *Punch* began to wane. Editors of newspapers began more and more to rely on the qualities of their humorous draughtsmen to sell copies of their papers. The Express group were particularly blessed as they employed that master of comic 'genre' scenes 'Giles', whose ever renewed comedy of family life dominated by a brooding 'Grandma' of Brünnhilde dimensions, has been much imitated, but never rivalled. The *Daily Express* was also fortunate in having on their staff Sir Osbert Lancaster, (born 1908), whose silky wit has illuminated so many fields from architecture to stage design. His innovative 'pocket cartoons' featuring the aristocratic Littlehampton family first appeared in 1939. We glimpse him at work here, however, in the more expansive mood of a menu for the Omar Khayyám dining club [plate 58].

Another master of the 'pocket cartoon' format is 'Marc', Mark Boxer (born 1931), whose pretentiously trendy Hampstead family, the String-a-longs, appear in *The Times*. 'Marc' is also a witty portraitist, with an eye for character as his drawing of Lord Goodman reveals [plate 59]. 'Marc's' first work appeared while an undergraduate at Cambridge, like that of the brilliant caricaturist of an older generation Edmund Xavier Kapp (1890-1978), whose incisive linear portraits included such varied figures as Picasso, Matisse, Shaw and Elgar, and an impressive series of great legal figures, like the famous barrister Sir Marshall Hall, [plate 60].

59
'Marc' Mark Boxer (born 1931)
Lord Goodman as 'Arnold Fatman'
Pen and indian ink, corrected with white
21.4 × 30.4 cms
E 680-1975
An illustration to Clive James's epic poem *The Fate of Felicity Fark in the Land of the Media* London, 1975.

60
Edmund Xavier Kapp (1890-1978)
'Sir Edward Marshall Hall K.C.'
Colour lithograph
An incisive portrait of the great defence counsel from a series of caricatures of legal celebrities published in *The Law Journal*, 1925.
28 × 22.7 cms
E 1633-1929

58 (opposite)
Sir Osbert Lancaster C.B.E. (born 1908)
Design for the Menu of the Omar Khayyám Club's Dinner held at Kettner's Restaurant on 25 November 1954.
King Farouk slips away from the back door of a Grand Hotel, on the Riviera, while Onassis, the Greek shipping multi-millionaire arrives in his Rolls-Royce—an ironic comment on the transience of wealthy playboys.
Pen heightened with white
38.7 × 28.3 cms
E 149-1969

The Animated Cartoon

Inevitably, in this concise survey, it is only possible to indicate certain rich seams of original work from the protean creations of this ever novel medium. But some mention should be made of the technique of animation, which, by imparting movement to static drawings, has enabled the art to take off in yet another direction, and brought yet another new meaning to the word 'cartoon'. While Walt Disney stands supreme in this field, much rewarding work has been produced by British studios, represented here by Halas and Batchelor's *Animal Farm* which in the 1950s brought George Orwell's satirical fable before a wide public [plate 61].

61
John Halas (born 1912) and Joy Batchelor (born 1914)
Two Pigs
Original art-work from the animated cartoon film
Animal Farm, based on George Orwell's satire.
Opaque gouache on talc
23.7 × 31.7 cms
E 554-1981

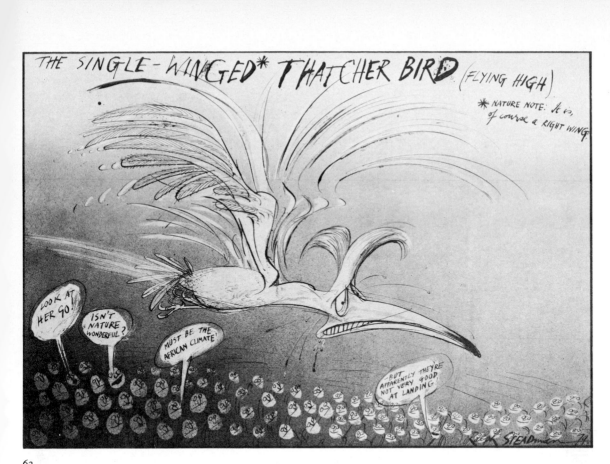

62
Ralph Steadman (born 1931)
Single Winged* Thatcher bird (Flying High)
*Nature Note: It is of course a Right Wing
Signed and dated R. Steadman '79
Pen, lithographic inks, chinese white
59.4 × 84.2 cms
E 5-1981
Reproduced in the *New Statesman* 31 August 1979

Private Eye

Perhaps the most important innovation in British satirical caricature since the War has been the foundation of that scourge and delight of the 'establishment', *Private Eye*, which has recently surprisingly celebrated its twenty-fifth anniversary. In its uninhibited pages a new generation of draughtsmen, notably Timothy Birdsall (1936-63), Gerald Scarfe (born 1936) and Ralph Steadman* (born 1936) has arisen with a venomous power

*They have all, of course, worked for other journals.

that harks back to the pungent savagery of Gillray. They share in common a gift of distortion for comic purposes which can almost produce physical nausea. Ralph Steadman's *Thatcher Bird* [plate 62] of 1980 takes its place in a tradition of satirical portraits of political leaders which stretches back to Gillray's diminutive Boney, the Corsican Ogre, and Philipon's epicine, pear-shaped Louis Philippe.

With new distorting images of this calibre the future of the caricaturist's art seems assured.

Where to see Caricatures

The British Museum's Print Room appropriately houses the most comprehensive collection of British caricatures from the age of Hogarth to that of Cruikshank, which has been magisterially catalogued by F. G. Stevens and Dorothy George.

The Victoria and Albert Museum's collections are, though not so comprehensive, more eclectic and diverse, containing, as this book indicates, many surprises. They can be seen in the Print Room.

Unlike most subjects covered in this series it is relatively easy for anyone, even of limited means, to form their own collection of caricatures.

Several dealers have in recent years opened specialised galleries in this eminently collectable field, and it is also well worth while paying regular visits to the stalls in the Portobello Road.

The editor of *Punch* will pass on requests for original artwork to the individual caricaturists whose work appears in that journal.

Further Reading

Ashbee, C. R. *Caricature* London, 1928
  Some unusual insights into the subject from an unexpected author, the famous Arts and Crafts designer.
Croft Murray, E. 'Venetian Caricatures' in Blunt, A. *Venetian Drawings of the 17th and 18th Century in the collection of Her Majesty the Queen, at Windsor Castle* London, 1957
  The best account of Ghezzi and his school by an enthusiast steeped in knowledge of the period.
Feaver, W. and Gould, A. *Masters of Caricature* London, 1981
  An invaluable dictionary.
Gombrich, E. H. and Kris, E. *Caricature* London, 1940
  The best concise book on the subject
Gombrich, E. H. *The Cartoonist's Armoury* in *Meditations on a Hobby Horse* London, 1963
  A stimulating assessment of the caricaturist's aims and motivations.
Hill, Draper *Mr Gillray the Caricaturist* London, 1965
  The definitive biography of the great caricaturist by a fellow caricaturist and scholar.

Houfe, Simon. *The Dictionary of British Book Illustrators and Caricaturists 1800–1914* Antique Collector's Club, 1978
  Far more than a dictionary—a lavishly illustrated history of the subject.
Low, Sir David *British Caricaturists, Cartoonists and Comic Artists* London, 1942.
  A great caricaturist describes his art and fellow artists. Low wields a pen as witty as his pencil.
Spielmann, M. H. *The History of 'Punch'* London, 1895
  Invaluable for its biographical material on the famous Victorian 'Punch' caricaturists.
Stevens, F. G. and George, M. Dorothy *British Museum Catalogue of Political and Personal Satires*, 12 volumes, London, 1978
  These grand volumes provide chapter and verse for the most obscure caricatures of the eighteenth and nineteenth centuries, but the knowledge they contain can be more conveniently assimilated in
George, M. Dorothy *Social Change and Graphic Satire from Hogarth to Cruikshank* London, 1967, the distillation of a lifetime's knowledge by a great scholar.